Once there was a Tadpole

For Jeremy - J.A

For Hannah, Carl, Heather
and little miss trouble! - M.G

First published in 2009 by Wayland
Copyright © Wayland 2009
This paperback edition published in 2012 by Wayland

Wayland, 338 Euston Road, London NW1 3BH

Wayland Australia
Level 17/207 Kent Street
Sydney NSW 2000

Editor: Nicola Edwards
Designer: Paul Cherrill
Digital Colour: Carl Gordon

The right of Judith Anderson to be identified as the
author of the work has been asserted by her in
accordance with the Copyright, Designs and Patents
Act 1988.

British Library Cataloguing in Publication Data

Anderson, Judith, 1965-
Once there was a tadpole
1. Tadpoles - Juvenile literature 2.
Amphibians - Life cycles - Juvenile literature
I. Title II. Gordon, Mike
597.8'139

ISBN: 978 0 7502 6736 6

Printed in China

Wayland is a division of Hachette Children's Books,
an Hachette UK company. www.hachette.co.uk

Nature's Miracles

Once there was a
Tadpole

Written by
Judith Anderson

Illustrated by
Mike Gordon

WAYLAND

Springtime is fun.
There are lots of new
things to look out for.
I look out for frogspawn.

Each egg has
a ball of jelly on
the outside, to
protect it.

The eggs stick
together.

My sister wants to take a little bit of frogspawn home.

But we don't take it from the river. We take it from our friend's garden pond.

After a few days we see a change. Each dot gets bigger and grows a little tail.

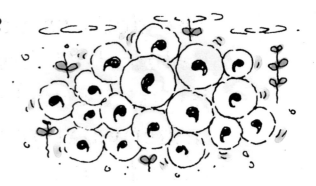

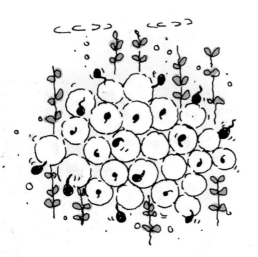

It wiggles its tail very hard, to push its way out of the jelly. It eats some of the jelly, too.

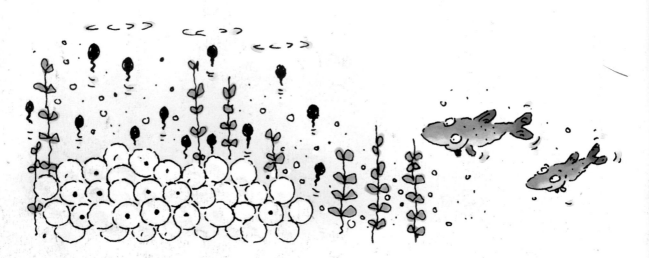

The dot has become a tadpole! At first the tadpole is just like a fish. It breathes underwater through little frills called gills.

But after two or three weeks its frilly gills disappear. Eventually the tadpole must swim to the surface to breathe in air.

Just like we do.

Tadpoles need to eat in order to grow. They use their tiny lips and teeth to nibble on plants in the water.

They need plenty
of food. They also
need clean water,
warmth and shade.

When the tadpole's body is the size of a fat pea, two bumps appear on its sides. Soon these bumps grow into back legs.

Then two more bumps appear.
Guess what these will grow into?

Now the tadpole is changing really fast. First its tail gets shorter. Its eyes start to bulge out and its mouth gets wider.

It starts to eat insects
and little worms.

Twelve weeks after
hatching out, the tadpole's
tail has vanished altogether.

It's time to put you back.

It looks like a little frog. Now it is called a froglet!

The froglet begins to climb
out of the water and spend
time on dry land.

After three years
it has finished
growing.

Now it is
an adult frog.

In the spring, the adult frog looks for a mate. He croaks to get the female's attention.

He's not the only one!

The female frog lays her eggs in a sheltered place in the water, and the male frog fertilizes them.

Next spring we'll go looking for frogspawn again. And the frogspawn will hatch into tadpoles again. And the tadpoles will change into frogs again!

It's a life cycle - a life story
that goes round and round,
over and over again!

NOTES FOR PARENTS AND TEACHERS

Suggestions for reading the book with children

As you read this book with children, you may find it helpful to stop and discuss what is happening page by page. Children might like to talk about what the pictures show, and point out the changes taking place in the young tadpole and froglet. What other changes can they see?

The idea of a life cycle is developed throughout the book, and reinforced on the final pages. Ask the children if they know of any other life cycles. Can they see any patterns in nature? The other titles in the series may help them think about this.

Discussing the subject of tadpoles and frogs may introduce children to a number of unfamiliar words, including frogspawn, gills, mate and fertilize. Make a list of new words and discuss what they mean.

Nature's Miracles and the National Curriculum

There are four titles about cycles in nature in the **Nature's Miracles** series: *Once There Was a Tadpole*; *Once There Was a Seed*; *Once There Was a Caterpillar* and *Once There Was a Raindrop*. Each book satisfies a number of requirements of the Science curriculum at Key Stage 1, and encourages children to explore the natural world for themselves through direct observation and specific activities. The books emphasise developing a sense of responsibility towards plants, animals and natural resources.

Once There Was a Tadpole will help young readers think about where and how tadpoles and

frogs live in the world around them, in line with the unit on 'Plants and animals in the local environment'. The book provides learning and discussion opportunities for units on 'Variation', 'Habitats' and 'Life cycles' by introducing the idea that frogspawn, tadpoles and frogs require specific conditions for survival and reproduction.

Suggestions for follow-up activities

The children in this book take a small amount of frogspawn home and place it in a suitable tank where they can watch the tadpoles develop. Rearing frogspawn at home or in school enables children to observe for themselves the process of change (or metamorphosis) that takes place and encourages a caring attitude towards wildlife. Only take frogspawn from a garden pond, as this will be less invasive to the natural environment. The conditions in which you keep frogspawn need to be monitored carefully:

• Use fresh rainwater or water taken from the pond – not straight from the tap. If the water turns brown and murky, replace some of it with fresh pond or rain water.
• Provide some pond weed for young tadpoles to cling to, feed from and shelter under. Remember that older tadpoles need more than weed to eat. Try a little fish food.
• Make sure the tank or pond is not in direct sunlight – some shade is best. Cover an open tank with netting to deter predators.
• Provide a flat rock so that froglets can crawl out of the water.
• Release them back into their original habitat before they are big enough to hop away.

A note on health and safety: Water presents many potential hazards for children. They should always be accompanied by a responsible adult when investigating ponds and streams.

Books to read

Popcorn Life Cycles: Frog by Ruth Thomson
(Wayland, 2009)
Learning about Life Cycles: Frog by Ruth Thomson
(Wayland, 2009)

Useful websites

www.ypte.org.uk/docs/factsheets/env_facts/frogspawn_tadpoles.html
www.oum.ox.ac.uk/thezone/animals/life/produce.htm

Index